We Know the Owner
A tribute to restaurant workers, because we deserve it.

Carlee Antonia

Cover by: Alec Conwell

@sincxrxlystars

Copyright © 2020 Carlee Antonia
All rights reserved.

Contents

"Hi, I'm Carlee, I'll be Helping You Out This Evening" 7

Let Me at It 11

Being The 12-Year-Old Boss 21

Stick Up For Yourself 31

Alone Time 35

I Like It Here, Thanks For Asking 39

We Are Not Getting Dumber 43

"Sure" 49

Sir, Please Remain Calm 59

Drawing a Line 71

Go Make Some Friends, Won't You? 75

You Missed a Spot	81
Shooting for Five Showers a Week	85
Sometimes I Fire Myself	91
So, You Know The Owner?	97
Restaurants Are Like Playgrounds	101
You Are The Weakest Link	109
This One's For You	115
"Any Coffee or Dessert for you Guys Tonight?"	125

Dedicated to my family's restaurant, and everyone that has ever called it home.

"Hi, I'm Carlee, I'll be Helping You Out This Evening."

This is not a self-help book. Although I do love myself a juicy, motivational, you can do it, aspiration-pushing self-help book. This is also not *How To Be a Waitress For Dummies*. Before sitting down for the first time and actually typing this here short novel, I made a list. The list contained all of the various strategies that I use to survive a day in the life as a restaurant manager.

The list was elaborate.

More elaborate than I had planned for it to be.

These tips and pieces of advice if you will, were so straightforward it almost felt dumb to write them out. You see, the restaurant industry is a rough one, sometimes a disastrous one if you are not careful. There are so many people that enter this line of work as a part-time side hustle and turn it into a full-time career, and then there are people who go at it full force and can't take the heat after a month. I have seen both. I have been both people. If you, like me, call or have once called yourself a server, bartender, busser, host, or manager of a food establishment, I applaud you, while simultaneously questioning your morals.

I know, just by the fact that you picked up this book, that you have some crazy in you. There is a part of who you are that craves the chaos that the food industry brings. There is something about this business that drew you in and held onto you for dear life. I empathize with and respect the shit out of you.

"Restaurant people", deserve a book (we also deserve new aprons and benefits, but I can't please everyone). We need this. Servers, bussers, hosts, bartenders, whoever you are in this industry, you deserve a handbook that you are proud of.

Why should corporate workers and entrepreneurs have guidelines and power-points on how to handle their daily jobs when we do not? So, I have written the damn handbook.

Here is all of the advice that I have on how to survive (*and thrive*) while working in a restaurant. This book contains complaints, triumphs, lessons, and stories that have been passed down from lifers to new hires over and over again. My intention here, on these pages, is to share my experience. To bring all of us food industry workers/goers/owners together in this safe space to relate to one another.

Restaurants are insane, weird, loud environments that not everyone has the "pleasure" of working in. The sole purpose here is to help you to feel like someone else gets it. Someone else out there hates their job on some days but would do almost anything to save it from going under. Someone else's best friends are their co-workers and their regulars know all their dirty secrets. Someone else knows what it's like to run around all night to please people that sometimes only leave a 10 percent tip and a mint.

This business has brought to light, my true colors, values, and capabilities. The food industry will do that to ya. Bring out your ugly, bring out your motivation, and bring out your physical ability to carry five water glasses at a time.

It has shown so many of us that we are a lot more or less patient, friendly, fake, or calm than we previously would have believed. This career takes a lot more skill, talent, and drive than society gives us credit for and that is why I am here. To lend a hand to anyone in this industry who is trying to keep it together, and to help those who do not work in restaurants understand that, this too, is a respectful profession.

I hope that you find comfort in knowing there are a million other people out there as crazy as you are for choosing the food industry as a source of income. Whether you are here for some advice, a sense of community or a laugh, welcome. Happy reading, Let's eat.

Let Me at It

In September of 1999, my family opened an Italian BYOB. Having little to no idea that this momentous event would ultimately decide my future as an entrepreneur, five-year-old me stood back and took it all in. The long hours, the brainstorming, the money, the menu… everything being stitched together and constructed right in front of my little eyes. All I could swallow at the time, was the fact that my dad was way cooler than the other dads because he was a pizza man.

Being in kindergarten when my family was building the business, I quickly became accustomed to restaurant talk and the fast-paced energy of the food business. It became clear to me, at an early age, that people who worked in this industry were a special breed. These unique individuals that chose chaos and uncertainty over a "nine to five," have never been anything but normal to me. Servers, chefs, takeout girls, bussers etc.…anyone who has worked or currently works in the restaurant industry understands how that statement is absurd, of course, we are anything but "normal." We are a rare group of workers. A diverse, fast-moving, multitasking, cash-loving pack of weirdos that I have grown to cherish so much.

    I grew up with an unusual amount of curiosity when it came to my family's restaurant and would do almost anything to spend time inside its walls. Standing only three feet high, my wide brown eyes gawked at the teenage bussers and seemingly mature waitresses. My tiny head constantly tilted back to glance up at the magnificence that was and still is, our restaurant, our comfort zone, our warm-toned, second home.

    Many of my earliest memories are inside of the restaurant; my mom picking me up and plopping me down on the meat freezer, bending down to my eye level and whispering, "Guess what?" looking at me with excitement, waiting for me to show her excitement back, "you're going to be a big sister again!"

"Yay?" I faked a smile. I'm sure I was excited but to be honest, all I cared about at that moment was getting off that meat freezer so I didn't look so young and childish in front of the people I thought were my co-workers. I constantly longed for their approval. The 60-year-old waitress or the 16-year-old dishwasher, it didn't matter. They were a part of my dad's creation and therefore, they were cool.

At seven years old I was in my happy place, wandering in and out of the buzzing kitchen. Believing I was small enough to go under the server's legs in an attempt to be less annoying as they worked around me. I craved the loudness, the screeching of the pizza oven door, and the deafening sharpening of the kitchen knives. Everything and everyone there was larger than life.

I recall my dad speaking a language I didn't know he spoke to these hustling, energetic men that would pump out beautiful food faster than I could tie my shoes. I was starstruck.

Standing on a chair with ninety percent of me covered in flour, I learned how to flip small pizzas in the air and started thinking I had some type of talent. When the cold dough was almost too heavy for me to pull apart, I would lie that I couldn't do it, just to watch my dad's big, rough hands make the pizza with ease.

He was and still is superman in my eyes. He knew everything about food, about people, about work and about life. I would shuffle my small feet, and pick up my pace as I followed behind him as a kid, to make sure I didn't miss anything he said, for I took everything as a lesson. I became a sponge. My eyes absorbed every move he made, every dollar he counted, every dish he cooked.

Looking back, my dad would most definitely tell you that I was a quiet child however I was only quiet around him, in an attempt to copy and paste his every move.

My dad was only one of the aspects of the business that drew me in and held me close as a young kid. The feeling of belonging, the satisfaction of being treated like an equal by servers who were so much more mature than I. It all made me want to be a part of the food industry more than anything else. I was spending so many hours at the restaurant that to this day, it barely feels like a job at all.

As a kid, I remember believing the servers were professional athletes and the busboys were way out of my league. Everything in the restaurant seemed cool. Everyone seemed so intelligent and motivated to elementary school me. They had a sureness about themselves. The way they talked to customers and remembered everything without writing anything down. Their middle fingers typing on the touch screen computers so quickly it made me dizzy. I had little to no clue about the amount of energy, time, money, blood, sweat, and tears that went into a place like this. I watched hours go by like minutes, getting in everyone's way and just wanting so badly, to be a part of the chaos.

"Carlee, go sit down."

"Carlee, why don't you go into the dining room? We're really busy."

"Carlee, maybe you can help out another day, today is crazy in here."

Little did they know that I gave absolutely zero shits.

The word "busy" only got me hyped up. How small I was never fazed me, neither did the fact that I was getting burned by spilled coffee every time I tried to help in the kitchen.

My admiration for these people was so gigantic, I would frequently forget that I was only a kid. I would arrive at home with oil stains all over my t-shirt and only want to go back for more.

As the years flew by, my desire to be a part of this place only grew stronger. I couldn't wait to get my hands on a piece of dough or a bar towel and just go at it. I wanted in. Being one of these people was more to me than just working my first job, it was joining my dad's legacy. It was becoming an adult, a big person with big responsibilities and it was making my dad proud. It was learning all the tricks and gaining all of the skills that the older servers already had. I was going to be one of them, part of their family, part of their clique. Little did I know this would be the beginning to the end. My first true love and my forever home.

When I turned 11, my dad gave into my years and years of begging and allowed me to start bussing tables. This was probably illegal, seeing that I most definitely did not have working papers at the time and was learning how to open and pour wine before I could drive. I figured out very quickly how to multitask and listen to authority. How fascinating it was to watch the servers, bussers, hosts, and counter people work as a unit to make the operations of the restaurant run smoothly. I gawked at *everything*. I would find myself staring at the managers as they set up and broke down tables faster than the bussers and the waitresses seat tables for the hosts. They worked together, as a team.

These people were animals. Running and sweating and carrying glasses and occasionally arguing and laughing over ridiculous requests. Floating back and forth between tables full of guests, ringing in orders, and solving problems, everything about them was wild to me. Over my first couple of years of employment, I came to admire the manic environment that is an Italian restaurant. The unending rush of the food industry is something that always had and always will have my heart.

What I have learned over the years, through careful observation, is that a dinner shift in a place like my family's restaurant can go one of two ways. The first way looks like five hours passing by in a calm, moving wave, maybe the dining room is cool and collected, customers are trickling in, and there is a steady flow of entrees coming out of the kitchen all night long. The second way a dinner shift might go looks like stepping into a frat house, without the keg stands or stench of Natty light. I prefer to call these nights "tornado nights." They are reckless and frantic. Every customer has a two-year-old that is screaming and all of the wine glasses are breaking. Every waitress is on the verge of tears and the credit card machine has overheated.

Sound fun? To the people that are thinking yes or possibly getting lit up over the idea of a tornado night, I feel you. We live for this shit.

Restaurant people, as I have previously stated, are anything but normal. It is the absurd franticness of hectic nights that turn us on and keep us coming back for more. Getting metaphorically punched in the face by my first reckless shift, I thought, "This is my place." It was then, at the age of 12, that I subconsciously, unwillingly bound myself to my family's restaurant. I wanted it all.

As I got older, I thoroughly enjoyed hearing feedback from customers and watching their eyes widen at the sight of garlic rolls. The odd sounds they would make when the hot bread hit the table and the raving compliments they would dish out after paying the bill. Just watching hours of hard work roll by like minutes was not enough for me.

I made a promise to myself. I was going to run this place, and I would put everything I have into the success of my second home. I wanted the connections with regulars and wanted the reviews. I wanted the hours and the bread oven burns that came with it. Being fully immersed in the restaurant was the only way I would be satisfied. Feeling the rush of the hot air from the opening of the oven door, having the sharp scent of garlic hit me like a brick wall upon entering the restaurant. I lived for it. All of the cozy, comforting feelings that the place brought me and the thrill of the hectic, reckless nights. Everything was fast-past and magical and I wanted more. And more is exactly what I got.

Being The 12-Year-Old Boss

I am 26 going on 12. If you have never seen me in person, which most of you have not, here's a little preview. I am 4'11" and have a serious case of baby face. I haven't quite changed physically since the 8th grade and the only way you can really tell my age is by having a conversation with me. Going through school I was always one of the smallest students in my class, constantly getting picked up (literally) in the hallways by various men, boys, friends, and even strangers; joking that, "you're as small as my seven-year-old sister."

Now, looking like a kid is not ALL bad. As I have heard hundreds of times, "Oh, hun, that's a *good* thing, you'll be so happy when you're older!" - every middle-aged-woman I have ever had a conversation with.

As a kid, I didn't really mind being short as hell and consistently underweight. I had big opinions that made up for my short stature as well as a bunch of friends who could reach shit for me when necessary. I consistently asserted my opinions into conversation and talked rather loudly to make sure everyone around me knew I had something to say.

At the time, I did not realize how much my appearance would affect the way I was treated in the working world. I mean, who is thinking about the "working world" when you just got your learner's permit and had your first beer? That being said, it did not take long for me to realize that the way I looked would become problematic for me after graduation.

As a matter of fact, it took me about a week after starting back at the restaurant full-time to understand that I was going to face a whole new set of obstacles. I was and still am frequently called sweetie at the grocery store and hear, "awe she's so cute," when escorting customers to their table at my own restaurant. From the many furrowed brows and confused looks I received after telling people that I was in charge, I came to the realization that unfortunately, being taken seriously in this world has a lot to do with how a person looks.

I was used to being asked for a second form of ID when it came to buying alcohol, and I was used to the questions about high school after I had already attained my college degree. What I was not used to was people treating me differently and with less respect because of my appearance when it came to my job.

Once, I had a man tell me, with a laugh, "you cannot possibly be the manager, you little thing, you're not a day over 15."

It is not at all fair that people take a glance at me and ask to speak to my manager when I am in charge.

That's right, "how old are you?" has become a frequently asked question in my life, and while most people hate being asked about their age because they are afraid of looking old, I hate it for the opposite reason.

"Oh my god honey, you could pass for a middle schooler..." and "...wow my ten-year-old and you are the same size!" are not friendly ways of complimenting someone. It can be hurtful, degrading, and embarrassing to be repeatedly questioned about my age as if it has anything and everything to do with how capable I am at doing my job.

As I began to take on bigger roles at work with more maturity and responsibility than I was used to, I started to lose confidence in myself because of how I looked. I barely spoke up when I needed to; I felt awkward and uncomfortable being "the boss" of a group of people, and I was stuck in the mindset that I was smaller, younger, and not smart, educated, or skilled enough to take on a job that someone else could clearly do better than I could.

How could I possibly hire and/or fire someone when I couldn't reach the coffee filters? How do I delegate side work to a 35-year-old with two kids on my 24th birthday with little more than a hangover and a bachelor's degree? *I am 24, why would any of these employees listen to me when they are my elders?* My brain would tell me. *Maybe I shouldn't talk to them like that, they've been here longer than me* or *just let it happen, they are older than me and they know what they're doing.*

I realize now that the way I looked affected how *I* thought about myself more than it affected the way other people thought of me. When it came to holding a position of authority in the restaurant, the snobby comments and ignorant questions hurt my feelings, but not as much as my own criticism towards myself did. It took me one too many years to learn to ignore people's questions, remind myself I am old enough and smart enough to manage a staff, and stand my ground when customers do not take me seriously.

I learned that anyone who runs a business is bound to hear some negativity. Whether that negativity is directed at the way a person looks or the way they run their company, it is almost inevitable that there will be some hate. Odds are, there will always be cranky old men that insist on speaking to "someone with authority here!" as they stare right through you. I have learned over the last few years how to interact with customers and people in general when they doubt my abilities to run a company.

Below, I have provided a short list on how to deal with these special people:

1. Remind yourself that they are close-minded and will probably have difficulty in their lives because of it.

2. Do not take the way that they view you personally. People who judge you and your abilities by the way that you look, do not know you in the first place. Therefore, their opinions do not matter.

3. Serve them their filet and let it be. No one gets to decide how capable you are in your life except you. It will cost you more energy trying to convince these people of the authority you have than to just let it go.

For a short period of time, I could not stand how young I looked. It was not until I learned how to really appreciate who I am in this industry that I began to gain confidence in my position of authority. No one enjoys hating themselves. And sometimes, in order to not hate yourself or maybe even love yourself (it is indeed possible), one must go through some shitty, negative, self-criticizing time to realize you're worth putting the work in. Telling yourself you are smart enough, skilled enough, and boss enough to run a company. Sticking up for yourself when you are being belittled or misjudged. Trusting your own opinions more than those of others. All of these tactics have helped me gain confidence in myself and my ability to run this restaurant.

Some people do not understand and might even be confused about why you have chosen this industry in the first place, so learn to let it go. You know what you are capable of, own it. Confidence is essential for management; without it, one will not be able to delegate responsibilities, reprimand poor performance, or hold any position of authority.

So many times I have had to stand my ground and find my inner confidence when dealing with judgmental customers. Although it is a skill that I am still working at, learning to stay confident has saved me many times when it comes to unfortunate interactions.

On a typical, busy Friday night, my staff and I were rushing back and forth from the dining room to the host stand to the computers, hot food being pumped out of the 90-degree kitchen onto the seemingly calm, intimate dining room. Frank Sinatra pandora station playing above the chaos, only to be heard if one took the time to listen.

Amidst swiftly moving to the soda machine to refill a customer's diet coke, a man grabs me by the arm, "Excuse me sweetheart, but where is Mr. Owner tonight?"

First of all, it is rude to touch me, sir.

I took a deep breath, genuinely pissed off that this man had just grabbed me, and annoyed that he assumed the owner was a man. "Sir, I am the owner, can I help you with something?" The fury in my face was most definitely noticeable as I attempted to be the bigger person.

"You are? No way!"

Taking another deep breath as my patience was being tested, "Is there something you need, sir?"

"I just wanted to let the owner know how great our meal was!" The man exclaimed with a slightly confused expression, still obviously unsure if I was being completely honest about my position.

"Thank you, I'm so glad you enjoyed everything," I replied as whole-heartedly as possible. "Let me know if you need anything else tonight."

As I walked away, I stood a little taller (reaching almost 5 feet and feeling a whole lot more confident).

Stick Up for Yourself

Just because you appear to be 12 years old, have opened a business at 65, or have nine kids at home does not mean you can't run the shit out of your company. I've had plenty of customers dumbfounded by the fact that I run a restaurant and that I am doing an above-average job. Whether that be because they initially thought I was in middle school or that I am a female or both, their opinions do not matter. I have learned to tell them who I am, know my worth, and serve them the best damn gnocchi vodka they will ever have.

A few weeks ago, I was running around like a madwoman, helping serve food, entering in takeout orders, and cleaning tables when a man raised his eyebrows and hand simultaneously to get my attention.

I shuffled over, bar towel in hand, ready to engage in whatever this man was about to ask of me. "Can I help you, sir?"

The well-kept, 60-something gentleman, looked at me with a slight smile, "Is that your boss over there?" he asked in a slightly higher tone than his normal speaking voice, as if he was speaking to a child. He pointed over my shoulder.

I looked back and to my surprise, it was my 18-year-old busboy, Justin.

Justin. The busboy who worked one night a week and was still in high school.

As I attempted to keep my cool, I replied, "Sir, I am that boy's boss. If you need anything, I'm sure that I can help you out."

The man was quiet in his disbelief. I cleared the dishes off his table as he stared at me, confused as to how I could possibly be in charge of anyone, seeing that must only be a teenager.

I walked away with nothing more out of the customer than a bewildered expression. About twenty minutes and a wave of new customers later, the same man called me over again. Enough time had passed that I had started to forget about his absurd question. Heading towards his table for the second time brought back my frustration.

A wave of anxiety rolled through me. "Yes?" I calmly smiled.

The man glanced down, then up at his wife and then over to me.

"That was very sexist of me to think that that boy was your boss when you clearly know what you are doing, I was raised better than that and I am sorry." He glanced down in embarrassment.

I was shocked. Also, extremely appreciative that this man owned up to his mistake and apologized for making assumptions. I have found, in this industry, that when someone disrespects you, even if it is unintentional, the tension will stick around until that customer leaves. However this man, after owning up to his mistake, taught me to not take assumptions to heart. I appreciated his apology so much that he quickly became one of my favorite regulars.

Alone Time

One of the first lines of my "how to survive the food industry" list stated "have alone time". It was high up on the list for a reason.

The first summer of "freedom" after college taught me many things, but nothing as important as how to be alone.

Spending an average of fifty hours a week catering to people who need their cokes refilled and more syrup in their kids' chocolate milk, you become a good multitasker, not necessarily a good person.

The ways in which I became a better person had little to nothing to do with how fast I could run through the restaurant carrying hot plates. I had to make time for myself. What an awful sounding idea it was at first. But I did it. I took the time to journal, meditate, practice yoga, listen to music, and journal more.

What I have learned through all of this is that without taking care of myself, I could never do my job effectively. And in the times that I do not feel like taking a break or exercising or writing, that is when I need it the most.

This industry is brutal. As many people who have worked in the food industry for a long period of time will tell you, you rarely have time to look in the mirror, let alone figure out what makes you happy. This job takes your nights, it takes your social life, and it takes your good hair days.

The food business will make you feel like a millionaire one week and put you in debt the next, and in no type of consistent pattern. The regulars turn into your closest friends and the customers you hate are always the most frequent to come in to eat. I have smelled like garlic at parties with cute boys and have had a piece of spinach in my hair since '06. Like I said, brutal. And personally, it's a hundred times more exhausting if I have zero time to decompress from all the bullshit, and zero time to wear my hair down once in a while.

So, take time for yourself.

It could be before you start your shift, right when you get off the clock, or even at 3 a..m. as long as you give yourself ten minutes alone. That's ten minutes without your phone or tv or a customer yelling at you to reheat their pizza; ten minutes alone can make a world of a difference in your life.

Devoting a minimum of ten minutes a day just to myself, changed the way I manage my staff, respond to customers, and handle problems. This time will literally reset your brain, give your body a physical break, and calm you down emotionally. Working in a restaurant full-time or honestly even one night a week can take a lot out of a person. It can drain you physically, mentally, and emotionally. We deserve downtime as much as the next workaholic and without it, going certifiably insane is not a very far-fetched possibility.

It took me a long time to realize that I deserve time off and that, without it, I can not function properly during the time that I am working. So take the time to be with yourself. ALONE. I promise you, it will only make you a better person when it comes to those long hours at work, surrounded by hungry customers.

I Like It Here, Thanks For Asking

Top 5 Most Ignorant Questions To Ask a Server:

1. What are you going to do with your degree?

2. So, what do you do other than this?

3. Do you want me to see if my job is hiring?

4. Do you need help with your resume?

5. Are you tired?

Customers can be rough. Let me rephrase, customers WILL be rough.

I have had a customer leave me her email address with a note attached, "Send me your resume, I know someone who is looking!"

Some people have no boundaries.

Oh, how will one ever survive? How will we make a living here at this food establishment? How will we teach our children to reach for the stars when we are "only waitresses"?

For at least an entire year, I struggled with the feeling that I was not smart or capable enough to have a job other than serving. Instead of recognizing how difficult and demanding my serving job was, I was putting myself down for not working in a field that required a degree, even though I had one. A lot of this doubt stemmed from being asked by customers why I went to school, got my degree, and then continued to serve tables. The rest of the doubt simply came from my own self-consciousness. If i am paying student loans, shouldn't I be using my degree and working in an office? After spending four years at school shouldn't I get to wear pant suits to work?

I couldn't fight myself any longer.

Shortly after my college graduation, I came to the realization that I was still madly in love with my family's restaurant. I found myself slipping away from everyday life to spend ten minutes immersed in the inside jokes and commotion of the restaurant staff. The subtle warmth and sense of community inside those walls calmed me down and got me inspired simultaneously. I wanted all of it, even with my semi-pointless college degree. I longed to do what I was good at and to make money doing it. So I chose to go all in. I picked my battle, I began working in the restaurant full-time and I've loved (almost) every minute of it.

For those of you who have made a restaurant job your full time gig, listen closely...just because we work weekends, late nights, and clean off dirty plates, does not mean we are not motivated. We are making money and supporting ourselves and doing a damn good job. Thick skin is required for this line of work and if you don't have it now, best believe you will grow it soon enough. Figure out what it is that you want most in this world, and then never explain yourself. You will never please everyone.

I have come to the conclusion that I will never convince Susan at table ten that working in a restaurant is also a career, just like her office job. You do not have to explain to the man eating his cannoli why you do not want to get your Real Estate License. Do not allow these people to make you feel less than. Do not let people who do not support your dream, try to tell you what your dream should look like.

We Are Not Getting Dumber

My friends, when it comes to working in a restaurant, please remember… the stupidity of others will not, in fact, make you more stupid.

I completely understand being unable to focus or pay attention when out to eat in a crowded place. Busy dining rooms could cause anyone to lose focus and skip over parts of the menu. However, when repeatedly asked what type of pasta comes with the PENNE Pollo Rosa, a server's patience is bound to wear thin. I have had to teach myself to stay calm and remember that these customers were not born in a restaurant like I was. They are normal. They do not understand that, in reality, there is no difference between capellini and angel hair.

If I tell them that penne comes with the Penne Pollo Rosa or that rigatoni is the pasta in the Rigatoni Bolognese, they may respond with "Ok good, just what I wanted" or "Oh I don't like that, I want spaghetti."

It is alright.

They are out to eat, they are not there to use their reading skills in order to pick apart the menu. When they read 'vodka sauce' they might have even blacked out with excitement, so I cut them a break.

I do not let the reoccurring, dumb questions frustrate me, because believe me, they do not make me dumber and they will never end. Ever.

While we are on the topic, my next piece of advice: do not let *anyone* treat you like an idiot.

Let me reiterate, do not let anyone treat you like you are less intelligent than you are because you are serving them dinner. Many people who have not worked in the food business tend to have this mindset that we servers are servers because we are uneducated and, therefore, cannot attain another occupation.

Let us walk through a busy night in my restaurant together, shall we?

I enter through the front door to begin my shift and realize the restaurant is already packed with customers. *Typical.* Passing by the host, I hear a customer declare where he will be sat when there is clearly a list of people to be sat before him. The host shows a fake smile and attempts to calm the man down.

"Well then, put my name on your list! It's Tim, T.I.M!"

The host takes down Tim's request, unamused and tempted purposely spell it wrong.

I continue through the dining area; I pass the takeout counter, where a woman exclaims, "You said my pizza would be ready five minutes ago. It's not here! I want a full refund or I will not be happy." I watch as she checks her watch every thirty seconds scanning the restaurant to see if anyone else will help her.

"Ma'am, are you okay?" Thinking I am being helpful by asking. The woman replies, "I just need to be somewhere I don't understand what is taking so long."

I recognize that this is not an emergency. I assure her that her pizza will be out in a few moments and walk around the counter to help answer the three phone lines that are now on hold.

"Looks like they're understaffed," the aggravated woman mummers to other customers waiting in line.

Thank you, Ms. I was unaware that I have 40 ticket orders in front of me and only two hands.

At this point, I can already tell it's going to be one of *those* nights.

I take a deep breath and prepare myself for screaming children and broken plates.

Right before I get to the kitchen I hear a banging.

I turn to find a middle-aged woman, closed fists, banging on table 40 to get the attention of her server.

Appalled, I approach, "Ma'am, your server will be right over. There is no need to bang on the furniture." She then informs me that she was only doing so because her 3-year-old was hungry as if that was a valid excuse to act like an animal.

I find the woman's server, "Table 40 is ready to order. Warning, she's a rowdy one."

A type of Restaurant Bootcamp should be required to handle situations such as these.

Luckily, my staff is trained for this kind of nonsense. They do not argue, bicker, or become easily frustrated with difficult customers.

Instead, they follow the Three-Step Approach to Hangry Customers.

1. Sympathize with your customer to the best of your ability.

2. Smile, even if it must be forced.

3. Make their experience the most memorable that it can be (without letting them walk all over you).

Though some requests are absurd and unreasonable such as transforming the restaurant into a country club or changing the menu completely, my staff does their very best to understand the issue, respect the customers' feelings, smile, and carry on--solving any and all problems that are reasonable to solve.

This three-step plan of action applies to the most challenging situations in our industry; it will assist you when customers are banging on tables and help you to remain calm when you have four phones on hold. Use it in whichever situation calls for it because hell, I know there are a lot of them.

"SURE"

I have a customer named Emilia. She is around 85 and has used every one of her many precious years to become more and more displeased with life. Emilia orders an eggplant parmesan sandwich from us every week. Emilia is very consistent. Over the phone, Emilia likes to demand extra sauce and a toasted roll. She sends various friends, family members, and care-takers to our restaurant to pick up her sandwich for her every time she orders. They come in; tell us they're here to 'pick up for Emilia;' they receive the eggplant parm.

Then we wait for the phone call.

It usually takes 17-25 minutes for Emilia to call back, reaming. This little old woman is not afraid to get loud.

Here is a short list of the many complaints Emilia has blessed my staff with over the last few years:

"There is not enough sauce!"

"There is too much sauce!"

"The roll is not toasted!"

"The roll is too toasted!"

"The sandwich is not hot!"

"The sandwich is too hot!"

"The sandwich has too much eggplant!"

"The sandwich has no eggplant!"

"The sandwich is not what I wanted!"

"I wanted two sandwiches!"

We never seem to get it just right for poor Emilia.

She has even taken it so far to have her care-taker come in and ask for a free sandwich before she even tried the one we made for her. I am telling you, this woman is not stable. We have countlessly attempted and failed to figure out what goes on inside of Emilia's head.

Once, one of my employees said to Emilia's niece, "Please tell your aunt to stop ordering from here. She is never happy with her order and has attained more gift cards and refunds than we can count."

Emilia called the next week to order her sandwich.

She's a fighter. The world needs more strong-willed women like Emilia.

Anyway, either her niece never mentioned to her that we had requested she not call back, or Emilia simply did not care. I'll let you decide which of the two you believe.

My employees decided to put the "Sure" policy to use every time Emilia called from then on out. She was the perfect test for my employees to challenge themselves when it came to using "Sure" in sticky situations.

We had been using "Sure" for some time when faced with argumentative scenarios, and Emilia definitely presented us with a learning opportunity. We decided, as a team, no more refunds, no gift cards, no sandwiches with light sauce on half of them. Just "Sure," and make the eggplant. If (when) she calls back to complain, take a deep breath, listen to what she has to say and, "Sure" our way out of it.

Recently, one of my regular customers came in for dinner. I served him his Gnocchi Vodka and returned to his table a few minutes later to check in. He looked up at me and said, "Well, this dish is a lot smaller than it usually is and I'm still going to be hungry afterward." I had two options in my response to this man.

Option 1: Bang on his table and count his strands of pasta, telling him he has received the same amount of pasta that he normally receives. Tell him maybe he should worry more about the fact that his kids are opening and eating all the sugar packets than the fact that his Fettuccine Alfredo seems three strands short. Make him aware that it takes my bussers AT LEAST ten minutes to clean up after his family every time they come in to eat, and he should be grateful.

Option 2: Simply respond, "Sure." There are so many reasons to fight back, so many excuses to give this man a piece of my mind, but then there is "Sure."

Maybe this guy was completely out of his mind, maybe he was just having a bad day, or maybe we really did not put enough pasta in his entree for his liking. Whatever the case, accept that the customer is upset. Use your best judgment to solve the problem in both of your favors and move on.

After hearing his complaints, I tell him that mistakes happen, and if he is still hungry after his entree, I will make him another small side. Anything else will be an additional charge.

Look, every food establishment runs differently. Maybe yours never gives anything away for free or maybe yours doesn't charge for drinks, kids' meals, or extra meatballs. No matter the case, we all make mistakes. Cooks, servers, managers, customers, everyone on planet earth, you know the deal. We are not perfect. Do not argue about who is right and who is wrong, because odds are, neither party is going to budge on their standpoints.

I was having *a night*. One of the nights where all of my tables needed me at the same time and everyone was seemingly starving. I was telling my busser something along the lines of, "this guy keeps calling me over while I'm talking to other tables; it's so rude." I was rushing around and frustrated. My busser, one of my most personable employees, caught me by the arm the next time I walked by her and said something that changed my entire mindset, "When someone is rude to me, I just tell myself they are having the worst day of their life." She smiled at me and continued clearing and resetting tables.

I could not stop thinking about it. What a beautiful way of giving a stranger the benefit of the doubt. They might be having a midlife crisis, or they could just be a rude person by nature, we can never know. By giving a customer the benefit of the doubt, using "Sure" will be a lot easier.

I have found the term, "Sure" to be the most efficient way of controlling situations such as these. Using "Sure" will support you when it comes to these unruly customers. It will be the backbone for serving regulars who ask for a specific number of grains of salt on their filet and it will keep servers calm when the elderly couple tells them that they are stupid for taking lasagna off of the menu.

The word "Sure" is commonly used as another way to say, "I will do that because it will not hurt, harm, or impact me negatively in any way."

Now, we will learn how to use "Sure" in the food industry to raise our tip averages, lower our frustration, and even provide us with more time while serving an unruly and extremely needy crowd. Sometimes, we have to let them win. It hurts; however, entitled customers will always try to put us down. No matter how many times we make their kids' chocolate milk, it will never have the right ratio of chocolate vs. milk. Their soda will not be bubbly enough and their pasta will not be their definition of al dente. If I have a customer who wants four forks but wants them to arrive at the table one after the other and only on a certain plate, then that customer is a pain in the ass, but I do not lose my mind.

There are many options when it comes to my response to these kind of people, but the one that will top all the rest is "Sure."

Let's practice together, shall we?

Customer: "Can I have cold water with no ice?"

You: "Sure!"

Customer: "Can you reheat my soup, the soup that just burned the shit out of my mouth?"

You: "Sure!"

Customer: "Can we sit at the table next to this one so that the fan won't blow on us there,

but also turn the air down because it's hot in here?"

You: "Sure!"

You see, it is so much simpler to let it go and just "Sure" instead of argue.

Do not go into the kitchen and bad mouth, do not give out dirty looks. Just "Sure" and everyone's lives become a lot easier.

If what the customer is asking for is impossible to give them, "Sure" may not be the best way to handle the situation. If and when Emilia calls back and demands four free eggplant sandwiches, "Sure" would only cost you money. However, through extensive research and experience, my co-workers, employees, and I have found that "Sure" is the most surefire way to hold onto your sanity and your precious energy. I know your ego may be hurt and your anger will need time to settle, but please believe me. This one word has saved me endless amounts of time and frustration when it comes to dumb tasks and will hopefully be a lifesaver to you too.

Go forth and "Sure."

Bonus:

For the servers who like a challenge and a slightly higher tip; attempt throwing in a smile while you "Sure." If this is too much for beginners, I completely understand. Please remember that we are only human.

Sir, Please Remain Calm

I have seen both sides of the food service industry. The bad and the good, the wonderful and the evil. My brightest days and my darkest times have been spent in the same dining room. Some of my fondest and most trying memories have been made inside of my family's restaurant.

<u>The Good:</u>

- I have received a hundred dollar tip on a forty dollar check (happy birthday to me).

- I have attended the baby shower of one of my closest regulars.

- I have worked nights with 30% tip averages.

- I have served shifts with my closest friends as my co-workers.

The Bad:

- I have thrown a man out for calling me "A stupid business woman," because I would not give him a free salad.

- I have had two children throw up in my dining room during the same shift.

- I have slipped down the basement steps during sidework.

- I have almost cut my finger off twice in one week with the same knife.

- I have worked 65 hours in one week serving tables.

The Ugly:

- Calvin's Wife

I would like to introduce you to Calvin. Calvin and his wife, both well into their 80s, thinning hair, short stature, used to be frequent customers of mine. They were extremely quiet (for the most part) and easy to take care of (on most days). Until the day that Calvin's wife went haywire.

Now, you have to trust me on this one, I am the first person in the room to feel bad for another. I frequently make excuses for those that are doing wrong or acting out and I have a great amount of sympathy for a person who is suffering. In this particular case, I was not so empathetic. This woman was off her rocker, literally and figuratively. The two of them had just polished off an entire bottle of white wine and she was not sober by any means, leaning on the table, eyes rolling every which way. I walk into the dining area from the kitchen and hear this woman screaming, "Don't touch me Calvin, get your hands off of me!"

I immediately recognized that she was confused, seeing that Calvin was nowhere near her. The swaying elderly woman was no doubt in the wrong state of mind. Her facial features were squished together in anger and pasta sauce was dripping down the side of her mouth.

As I proceeded to the table to assist them in leaving, the woman pushed my arm away from her and yelled, "Do not touch me!" This woman was ready to fight. I told her calmly that everything was fine and we were just going to wrap up her meal so they could be on their way. As my small, 16-year-old, curly blond-haired bus girl attempted to help the two of them wrap up their food, Calvin's wife swiftly, open-handedly smacked my busser across the arm. She smacked her! I was furious, and honestly slightly impressed by the frail woman's strength.

As I turned to move towards Calvin's table to somehow handle the situation, I looked up and saw my dad heading over to the scene of the drama. Now, my dad is a big, loving, Italian, kind man, but when it comes to his employees he is papa bear first and foremost.

After seeing this mess of a woman strike our busser, my dad walked over to Calvin and whispered, "If you don't get your wife out of here, I will do it for you."

As humane as possible, my dad and boyfriend (who also happened to be there at the time), attempted to help the woman leave the restaurant, seeing that she was too intoxicated to walk on her own. They tried to hold her up and gently move her towards the door but the nasty little thing was not having it. She pulled and pushed away from them and attempted to hit her husband for making her leave.

I have heard many curse words, and a varying number of harsh, belittling sayings in the restaurant but nothing that compares to what came out of this elderly woman's mouth.

"Everyone is hurting me!" Calvin's wife screamed even though there was no one within a three feet radius of her. I felt my mouth gape open, hearing swear words that I had never heard before, let alone from a little old lady. "Everyone stop touching me!" she yelled in her high pitched, crackling voice.

Then, she turned and pointed at her frustrated, equally old, and frail husband, "Calvin, you are a bitch!" she snarled as the crowd went silent.

Calvin remained calm, this was not his first rodeo.

Halfway to the exit, and the woman fell--a slow, dramatic, had to put some effort into it, fall. She yelped, "You pushed me! Help! Don't touch me!" My dining room full of customers tried not to stare, but couldn't look away.

My boyfriend, who's always up for a challenge, tried to lift the small woman back up to a standing position and that's when she threw a mighty right hook, just missing his face.

After quite the struggle, my dad and boyfriend finally got the woman up, with no help from Calvin who remained cool as a cucumber, thanking everyone for their assistance.

Calvin and his lovely wife got safely into their vehicle.

She left us with a middle finger in the air and the facial expression of a terrifying witch.

The duration of this entire episode was only about fifteen minutes from start to finish, yet was a total energy suck.

So, as I said, good, bad and *ugly*.

I wanted to share Calvin and his wife with you for one of two reasons.

One, you can not let events like this ruin your day. This industry is forever moving and changing and this old-ass lady should not decide for you how the rest of your shift is going to go.

Two, this shit is hilarious. It is not often that you get violent with an 80-year-old woman.

The best part? Exactly one week later the happy couple returns.

You are just as shocked as I was.

I seat them close to the door and explain to Calvin that if they are to even think about causing a scene they would be thrown out immediately. Calvin tells me that he understands and is sorry about the last time. His wife, however, glances right over my shoulder, proceeds to ignore every word that I am saying, and grabs a menu from the pile on the host stand. I am not surprised, as I prepare myself for their chaos. Calvin gives me a knowing, apologetic smile, then proceeds to pull out a big ol' bottle of white wine.

It is after multiple shit shows such as this one with the old, elated couple, that I have decided to write down the ways in which I handle the crazies.

Three Ways to Handle a Dining Room Shit Show

1. **Save It For Later**

When faced with a screaming customer (even one over the phone. Especially the one on line three while the other two lines are ringing), focus on first assessing the issue from their point of view. This will help you to be less angry with the customer that you value so very much.

In Calvin and his wife's case, we had to recognize that this woman was senile and had a very low alcohol tolerance.

Next, take down their name and phone number and deal with it later. I know this sounds like putting off issues and procrastinating, which I am so very good at, but it's not.

Again, in Calvin's case, make them leave and bitch about it later.

In no world is it benefiting anyone to yell, argue, or attempt to solve problems in the middle of a dinner rush.

These things must be handled delicately, and not with children around flinging spaghetti. Call them back when you are calm, when you are alone, and when you can solve the issue with a clear mind. This goes for issues that may arise mid-shift with co-workers, customers, employees, etc., nothing good comes from an argument in an already chaotic space. Address the problem, find time to talk it out later. Whether that means giving out a gift card, taking an item off of a customer's bill or making time to call your angry co-worker after your shift, these issues are not to be fought over during lunch rush. Save it for later.

2. **Delegate**

For all of my managers and owners out there, when the restaurant seems to be screaming at you on a weekend night, delegate. Whether you are talking to bussers, food runners, servers or hosts, they are there to make money. If someone needs a refill and table six needs their meatballs, ask for help. When Calvin's wife begins throwing hands, ask for backup. While you handle a problem, ask your co-workers to handle the restaurant.

I used to believe that I could do it all, sometimes still believe this, and if I attempt to do it all, best believe it will all get done. I could run my restaurant with no servers if I wanted to and do everything myself but no one would ever come back to eat. The night would be a complete and utter mess.

You have employees and co-workers for a reason. If you see something that needs to be taken care of, instead of running extra fast to get there, grab a busser, ask for help. Split up tasks. Work together. One section is everyone's section and if one person is making money, we all are. So make sure everyone helps you out, it will save you energy, sanity, and a broken ankle.

The opposite is also true, if you see that a co-worker is running through the restaurant like their life depends on the bread that is burning in the oven, help them out. Run their drinks, run their checks, just help *them* to stop running. The more we all do for each other, the calmer the shift will go and the calmer the shift, the more sanity we hold onto.

3. **Laugh at yourself. Always.**

Laugh at your mistakes. Laugh at your co-worker's mistakes. Laugh at the customer who tells the same shitty joke every Wednesday afternoon. Laugh about the nice, calm dinner that poor Calvin thought he was going to have. Laugh at the fact that you worked sixty hours this week and are delusional.

Just enjoy. Because all of this is temporary and it is only a job after all. Without some humor, humiliation, and good fun there would be no purpose in what we are doing here. Compile a corny mental list of inside jokes between your co-workers, and laugh with the couple that comes in for only one side dish. Take nothing too seriously, even when your staff gets thrown around by a little old lady.

Drawing The Line

As a 26-year-old who runs a business, a busy Italian restaurant to be exact, I occasionally find it difficult to remain a boss when my employees are some of my best friends. It sounds perfect, having your best friend as one of your servers and your little sister's boyfriend as your pizza guy, but these things are delicate.

As a manager, my responsibilities include training, reprimanding, and possibly firing employees that I simultaneously treat like family. Relationships can be put in jeopardy; when favoritism and nepotism come into play, it can become difficult to decide between being a boss and being a friend.

In order to solve the Friend vs. Boss dilemma, I suggest the age-old technique: drawing a line.

It has taken time, but I have finally figured out almost exactly where I draw my line (the line could be drawn differently and in different places for different people). Over the years and after several incidents of crossing lines, I have gotten closer and closer to establishing boundaries.

I mean, before I became a boss, I had little to no boundaries. Did I stay out with my co-workers until the wee hours of the night… maybe. Was it me that won a twerk contest in front of my entire kitchen staff at a Spanish night club, it's possible. Fortunately, I have grown and most of the videos of that night have been deleted. I can honestly say that I now know how to have a good time and uphold my title of "Manager" with responsibility.

I love going out with my employees and dancing and letting loose, but I draw the line at staying out too late or closing down bars with them. I love getting together with my employees outside of the restaurant, but the restaurant comes first. I draw the line at closing early, skipping side-work or choosing to do anything that would benefit our social lives but hurt the wellness of the business.

There are just certain things that can not take place even when you are an "easy-going" employer.

Examples:

- If my employees have a glass of wine after work, the employee that is *about* to turn 21 does not drink.

- If my sister is working one night and forgets to do part of her closing work, she is made aware of it just like everyone else would be.

- Everyone is held accountable when it comes to the restaurant's well-being. Side-work and cleaning come before having a good time.

- If we go out after work, I do not get drunk, or let my employees make bad decisions on my watch.

It has been difficult enough to remain "the boss" as someone who is the same age as or younger than my employees. Not having clear yes's and no's to what I allow and do not allow would only make my job that much harder.

Figure out your boundaries and stick to them.

It's important to recognize the difference between being a friend and being a boss. As easy as it is to let them blend together, keeping them separate will only make things easier for you, your employees, and your business altogether. Deciding to go to the night club is one thing. Deciding to drink whiskey in excess and twerk on stage is another.

Draw a line... for everyone's sake.

Go Make Some Friends Won't You?

Speaking of boundaries; I am in a four-year relationship with my former busboy. Okay, so he was not my employee when we met, he was my dad's. He was a busser in my family's restaurant when I was in college, coming home on the weekends to serve, or host, or work whatever shifts I could get my hands on for extra cash. I would sneakily try to figure out what days he was working so that I could be there too. At the time, we were living completely separate lives and the restaurant was our common ground. We would flirt, like co-workers do, putting ourselves in the same part of the restaurant at the same time and pretending it was an accident.

Long story short, I won him over with all the years of slipping his tips in his back pocket at the end of our shift and making fun of how nerdy he looked in his tucked-in black polo. I went from harassing him as a joke to picking up shifts that I knew he was scheduled for. We didn't start dating until he was no longer working at the restaurant, but I continue to tell people that I fired him so we could be together.

It has been four years and I could not be doing what I am doing now without his support. We have gone from scrapping dirty plates off into the same trash can together to sharing an apartment and a life, which still blows my mind.

I realize now that in this industry, it helps to have a partner that has gone through it too, even if they only served or bussed tables for a little while. It is important that they understand this industry's unruliness and demanding hours. I know my boyfriend is only in it for the chicken parmesan, but I love him and thank him as much as I possibly can for letting me bitch, helping me run around, and telling me I can do whatever I put my mind to.

This network of supportive people in my life is the reason why I am still sane (most days). Support systems are key. If you don't got one, make one. Get all the people together who believe in you and who understand that you actually enjoy this crazy industry. Meet other people who love to serve, manage, run food, cook etc.... These people will save you from the horrible nights and help you celebrate the great ones.

Whoever they are, these are the people who will not question you about your seemingly useless college degree or school loans that sometimes feel like a waste of money. They will not expect you to have a "real job" because they understand that what you love is this and that having a 9-5 would drive you crazier than a ten top of middle schoolers.

These people may not be your family or your closest friends like mine (which I am very fortunate to have), but they are around. They could be your regulars, your co-workers, or other food industry workers at another bar or restaurant.

This job is not for everyone; actually, it's not for most people. It is for the brave and the motivated. The patient and the determined. We are strong, but we need support too.

So, find the people that are as crazy as you are and swap stories of horrible shifts. Tell someone about the time you dropped a hot pizza on a child, and laugh about it (story told in better detail by my boyfriend who indeed dropped the pizza). These people are your greatest strength and will help you succeed in every aspect of your life. They will help you make the most money and support you when you have none. They will watch your kids because they understand how valuable that Saturday night shift is. We might act tough and mighty, but we all need assistance at one point or another. So ask for help. Find the people that support and motivate you and never let them go.

Along with the support system, another necessary piece of growing as a person in your career is finding a mentor. EVERYONE needs a mentor! Whether you are at what seems to be the top of your game or at your rock bottom. Whether you are a server, a cook, a manager, a host...

find a mentor. You will only grow in your position by learning from people that are better at it than you.

I am lucky enough that my mentor also happens to be my dad, but for anyone reading this, your mentor can be anyone who is proficient at their job. Anyone who is making more tips than you are, or anyone that shows up to work with more confidence and drive than you have. As a boss, find the servers that have the most experience, have the best reputation, and make the most money and allow them to train your new employees. In doing this, you are giving your new employees an opportunity to learn from the best and you are giving the employees that have been with you forever the recognition they deserve for their hard work.

I have had meetings with my dad where I have started off in tears and left the office feeling better than ever before. I have had days where I can barely get a word out because he is trying to get all of the lessons that he can into one day.

Amongst other things, I have learned to roll dough, use a drill, fix a heater, and price a salmon special all from my mentor. I cringe *and* get excited simultaneously every time I hear my dad's bellowing voice, "Carlee, come here!" from the next room. My advice is to listen. Once you have your mentor, take in all the information that you can.

Your support system, your mentor, your co-workers, they want you to succeed. Make room for these people in your life, they are more important than you know!

You Missed a Spot

I'm sure all of my former and current employees reading this right now are going to roll their eyes, I can actually feel it happening. Regardless, this stuff is important.

How you care for your place of employment reflects the kind of employee you are.

How you treat your space, whether that be a busser station, a cubicle, or a couch, is a representation of how you feel about your job.

And by all means, if you hate that job, leave. Find something you love or at least something you like. It's easy to forget but, WE GET TO BE HERE.

If you would rather scroll through Instagram than clean up your workspace or go out binge drinking with your friends instead of making a wad of cash on a Friday night, that is okay!

However, if that is the case then please choose one over the other.

If you hate it, leave.

If you are tired of it, find something new.

If you find yourself not able to refill one more cheese shaker before you throw it at one of the cooks, maybe this job is not for you, AND THAT IS OKAY!

But if this crazy lifestyle is indeed what gets you going, then do everyone (including yourself) a favor and do it right.

If your job calls for you to clean the bases of the tables every night, then you clean those bases to the best of your ability every time you do it.

If you go to the bathroom mid-shift and see that the sink is dirty, clean it. It will thank you, the staff will thank you, I will thank you.

This is what having pride looks like. Pride is taking care of the spaces that you work and live in. Pride is treating your workspace like home. Being proud of the place that you work means giving it consistent respect. I know these tasks are repetitive and your side work list sucks, but think of it this way; we chose this. And only a very small number of people in the world would have chosen this as their source of income, so you have superpowers. You are a special kind of psycho and we need people like you so please go wipe something down.

I grew up in my family's restaurant almost more than I grew up in my own house. This place is not just a food establishment. To me and to many of my co-workers, this restaurant is home and I take pride in that. It is safe and it is friendly and it makes us a living. It is a place where we are completely ourselves and a place that we can turn to for support. Restaurant co-workers are so much more than co-workers. They are family. There is an unimaginable bond that exists between restaurant staff members. So remember how lucky you are. We may be sweaty and manic and only pay for things with one-dollar bills but we are at home. Be proud of where you work. Take care of your place and each other with pride and it will take care of you right back. Treat your food establishment with the same amount of respect that you want to receive and it will be reciprocated.

Shooting For Five Showers a Week

There is no way in hell that people can care for a food establishment (or any establishment at that) if they cannot take care of themselves. So, this is where I will remind everyone to shower.

You know exactly who you are.

Listen, I know you work doubles. I know you ran the length of the restaurant for twelve hours straight today and burnt off your eyebrow on the soup warmer. I get it. Matter of fact, I've done it.

But please, no matter how exhausted you are, no matter how many rolls were thrown at you during your shift, and no matter how many times you had to repeat your specials during the night, please shower.

Do not go into your next shift with the mindset that you are just going to get dirty all over again, so what is the point?

The point is that YOU ARE AT WORK.

I know I am talking to you like you are a stubborn five-year-old, but you will feel better if you look better, it's just the way our brains work.

When we feel confident and clean, we are more productive.

I know serving and bussing tables are physical jobs full of fast-paced tasks, but you deserve to feel good doing them. We are professionals even though we don't wear suits, so treat yourself like one.

I have had the pleasure of bringing up the topic in a recent staff meeting. I got mostly laughs and eye rolls in response, but I was not joking. Customers can tell if you're going on day five with no shampoo, so please do something about it.

Here, for you, I have created a personal hygiene list that will keep you looking and feeling brand new, and hopefully up your tip averages.

The Hygiene Checklist for Restaurant Employees

Basics

- Shower (at least 5 times a week)

- Brush teeth (did I really need to put that on the list?)

- Put on deodorant (before EVERY shift)

Intermediate

- Have mouthwash in your pocket while on shift (we are talkers)

- Give up your two-year-old, non-slip, serving shoes and buy new ones

- Put some effort into your appearance before you walk into your job

Advanced

- Floss (every day)

- Get your nails done (as needed)

- Buy new work clothes (when your serving pants are so faded that they are no longer black, buy new work pants)

About a year ago, I promised myself that I would start getting my nails done consistently. Could I afford it at the time? No. Did I have an hour to spare on my only day off? Not really. But looking down at my hands and feeling clean and put together makes me feel better about myself and gives me a confidence boost. So I do it. I spend the time and the money because looking put together makes me feel put together. Even when I am working 60-hour-weeks. It's little tasks like getting your nails done, washing your hair more than twice a week, and wearing clean work clothes (for the love of God please do not go for day three in that shirt) that make all the difference in how we feel.

Show people that you are there to make money and that you take your career seriously and those people will show you more respect (and tip you better!).

I am not saying that you need to look attractive to make money, I am saying that you deserve to feel good about the way you look.

The day I started dressing professionally to manage my restaurant, was the day I started feeling like an actual manager. Do not let the food industry keep you from cleaning up, dressing nice, and acting professionally. This is a career, after all.

Restaurants are places that employees can easily become comfortable, sometimes too comfortable. Would you walk into an office job or a sales position with a hole in your shirt? Would you feel okay sitting at your desk job with your stomach showing or your pants falling down? If not, then what is the difference between those places and your restaurant job?

The way you carry yourself, your mannerisms, your clothing, your cleanliness, are all representations of how much you care about your job.

Please think about that the next time you wear two different neon-colored socks when your dress code calls for all black, and for god's sake, if you are debating between showering before or after your shift, just do both.

Sometimes I Fire Myself

Times that I have tried to fire myself:

- After almost cutting my finger off twice in one week with the same knife.

- After having a customer send her pasta back twice because it was "cold," and then on the third attempt, telling me that she burned her mouth on it.

- After mopping the entire restaurant and then spilling the very-full bucket of dirty mop water all over the clean floor.

- After a woman asked me where she should set up her "tye-dye" station for her baby shower in our private event room.

- After hearing Johnny Cash's "Ring of Fire" three times in one shift.

Here's the deal, I loathe Johnny Cash.

If anyone feels personally offended and/or needs to stop reading I completely understand and I thank you for your time up until this point. But guys, I hate him. His voice, his music, his face I just can't do it and I'm sorry.

"Ring of Fire" plays in my worst nightmares and "I Walk The Line" is one of my only triggers. I am admitting to you this awful dislike of mine because it leads us to our next lesson. Welcome to *How To Work With Family Members 101*.

My dad loves Johnny Cash, you see. He thinks "Walk the Line" is a great song to eat dinner to and whole-heartedly believes that all of our customers would agree. One night, after a long dinner shift of screaming children, broken wine glasses, and misfortune, Johnny made his appearance. I was closing for the night, counting the drawer for the fourth time when I heard one of his god-awful tunes faintly playing through the speaker.

That was it.

I took it upon myself to get the 20+-year-old iPod that we use for music and delete every one of Johnny Cash's songs I could find.

I had finally won.

'Twas the greatest triumphs of my young life. Two weeks float by with nothing but easy-to-listen-to dinner music glowing from the speakers. Two weeks of good sounds, serenity, and calming Motown.

A Monday morning rolls around and I am completing my opening side work per usual and there it is…It came through quietly at first, only the base. Slow but sure enough, I recognized it. "The Ring of Fire," creeping through the restaurant.

But how?

I was defeated and furious. How could it be that my dad, a man who talks into his phone to text, had figured out how to put Cash's songs back on the iPod? Did he google it? Did he have an accomplice? I was flabbergasted and slightly impressed.

I began questioning my staff; one of them had to have assisted him or even done the deed for him. I got nowhere, and there was no chance that I was bringing it up to the boss. After all, my dad and I disagree on more than just "A Boy Named Sue." I have learned the hard way that fighting at work, especially with family members and especially when they are your parents is not likely going to do any good. We butt heads over certain restaurant policies and employee performances. We have little to no patience with each other when it comes to doing the bills and balancing the bank account. I have probably quit my job seven times in the last week while I have been arguing with him, but he is my rock. My dad has taught me and continues to teach me how to budget, how to handle customers, how to price specials and how to be successful in business. He has shown me with examples how to prioritize, how to solve issues during service and how to unclog the backed-up dishwasher (my favorite!). My dad tends to put more pressure on me than anyone else but this is how I have learned the business.

Oh, You Know The Owner?

Being the daughter of a man who knows every person in your county has its ups and downs. When I was little I thought it was super cool that everyone knew and loved my dad. He would walk into the restaurant and so many customers would call him over to talk or to rave about the food and ask him about the restaurant. My dad is a quiet guy, not showy or boastful. So it always was and still is amazing to me that he has made such an impact on so many people in our community. I truly did enjoy that everyone knew and loved my dad until I began hostessing at our restaurant.

"We know the owner," they would boast. My regulars, my first-timers, people from the area and people who have only read about us on Yelp. "We know him, we know the owner."

I was around 15-years-old when I told a seemingly nice, middle-aged couple that their wait would be around 45 minutes. The woman looked at me, glanced over to her husband as if asking for permission, and stated what I wish she had not... "but, we know the owner…".

First of all, *I* know the owner. *You* have met him once or twice. I am the one that works by his side 50 hours a week. I am the one who argues with him on a day-to-day basis and I am the one who knows he hates that I hate Johnny Cash.

Human beings, as I have learned, loved to feel included. Everyone wants a piece of the pie and certain customers feel the need to make it known that they are part of the family (or they believe that they are). The couple that I had been talking to did not personally know my father. Maybe they had met once or twice or they went to high school together or had a previous interaction, all of which are insignificant at this point.

Let us break this down together.

- If this couple indeed "knew the owner," then you would think they would know me, his first child.

- If this couple indeed "knew the owner," they would respect his business enough to sit down, shut up, and wait their turn like everyone else.

Long story short, you do not really *know* the owner. And if you do really *know* him, then leave him be. He is working. He is running the business that you are buying from so please do not use him as leverage to get discounts or shorter waiting times. Please, for the love of good food, I am begging you, *do not boast about knowing the owner*. Or the manager for that matter. No one cares, you see.

If you do, in fact, have a relationship with the people that run the business, great. But really, do not ask for attention. Come in, support the business, show that you care, and get on with it. We appreciate your support, truly we do. But, if you feel the need to tell your server that you need special treatment because you "know the owner," maybe just order takeout next time.

Restaurants Are Like Playgrounds...

The Top 5 Craziest Reviews About Our Restaurant

1. "They use canned sauce." (false)

2. "The waitresses are on drugs!" (definitely false)

3. "Their meatballs are *FAKE!*" (come again?)

4. "The host opened the bottle of wine that we gave her and then lost the cork, we collect corks, we will never be back" (I'm sorry?)
5. "This restaurant is a playground for the owner's daughter."

(ouch)

Running the Playground

On a typical Sunday afternoon in August, I found myself where I am every Sunday afternoon, arriving at the restaurant, greeting my staff, starting to get the place ready for the dinner rush. As I entered the dining room, however, the counter girl, looking extremely frazzled, waved her left hand to get my attention while she held the phone in her right hand against her ear.

"I am sorry sir, I couldn't hear you, can you repeat that one more time?" She pleaded into the cordless, now with her left hand placed on her forehead in disbelief. "Sure, one large vegetable pizza, anything else?" She looked mortified, so I stuck around.

After aggressively hitting the off button, my employee of five years looked up at me in disbelief with her hand still on her forehead, "After I asked that man to repeat his order, he screamed at me, 'Are you new there?! Why do you not know what you're doing?!' He wouldn't stop yelling; he's crazy."

I felt the fury in my face start to rise. It is one thing to say disrespectful things to me, but when customers mess with my employees I tend to have a bit of a temper. Some people call it "little man syndrome," seeing that I am only 4'11." I just call it being protective.

I am now waiting, very impatiently, for this man to arrive for his pizza. He enters the restaurant. I know it is him right away from the dedication in his step and the anger lines on his face. This man was mad about more than a pizza. Storming right up to the counter the man looks me directly in the eyes.

"Hi, can I help you?"

The angry man wastes no time, "What is wrong with you on the phone?! Can you not understand my accent? You asked me three times what I ordered, you do not know what you are doing!" Now his hands were flailing and those anger lines around his eyes were becoming alarmingly angrier.

"Sir, our phones are not the best and sometimes they are hard to hear over, did we get your order correct?"

"Yes, but this is ridiculous!" he barked back.

"So nothing is wrong with your pizza, or the price? You are screaming at me because my employee could not hear you over the phone?" I question as I place his vegetable pizza in front of him.

Ignoring the question, the man straightened his stance and demanded that he speak to a manager (about what exactly I am unsure, considering his order was correct and in front of him ready to eat).

"You are speaking to the manager, sir."

He laughed. Pushed the pizza back at me and, I kid you not, announced, "I am calling the cops!" as he let his attention-demanding fist bang down onto the counter top and stormed out of the place, pizza-less.

The cops. For an extra 15 seconds of inconvenience over the phone.

I can only imagine the phone call between this fuming man and a law enforcement agent.

"911...what is the emergency?"

"Hi, I ordered a pizza at an Italian restaurant and they couldn't hear me over the phone. They asked me to repeat the order three times."

"Sir, is this an emergency?…"

"LISTEN, I got to the restaurant and they had my pizza ready for me!"

"Sir, I'm not sure that this…"

"I need you to send someone over there!"

I mean, I was honestly hoping they would send a cop. Just to have a couple more people there to laugh about what just happened with us.

Several hours and no cops later I almost put the experience behind me. But, I should have known better.

Bright and early the next morning, I get a notification on our Facebook page.

Somehow I knew what I was about to find.

The fuming, out-of-control man had left a scathing full-page review. It was a page full of hate words detailing an incident that did not happen. The man wrote that he called and we made him repeat the order ten times. He claimed that we could not take his order because of his accent and that we hung up on him. All of these words were not true and therefore did not offend any of my staff until the end of the post. The man decided to really hit where it hurts and typed "This restaurant is a playground for the owner's daughter."

This was a new one.

I was taken back and deeply embarrassed. Not only was I offended that someone who did not know me, would insult me and my family's business on social media like that, but I was also hurt by the fact that others would see those words.

The angry pizza man's post brought up a lot of questions. If I had said less would he have been less upset? If I lied and told him I was a server and not the owner maybe he wouldn't have written that kind of thing?

For a few days, I was pissed off and confused. I couldn't help but to imagine the scenario in my head and question if I had handled it the right way. Would my dad have done the same thing? Would my servers have reacted in a similar way? If I was older looking, maybe he wouldn't have talked down to me like he did. If I was a man would he have even fought back or called me names on social media?

A few days after the incident, I was running appetizers to a table of happy guests when I paused and glanced around. My dad was joking with a couple that has been coming into our restaurant for years. My servers and bussers were mid-debate about something irrelevant and inappropriate, poking fun at each other. It dawned on me that, no matter the occasional angry review, we are good people, with good intentions.

People who know my family and I know that we are kind people. You can not defend yourself against people who do not know and do not care to know who you are. I am who I am and I am that person because of my family and this business. I have learned to never apologize for what I believe in and to consistently stand up for myself. Even if sometimes, standing up for yourself hails you a shitty tip or an aggressive Facebook post, remember that not all people are cruel and we are all in this playground together.

You Are the Weakest Link

Here is the thing about managing employees, it is both wonderful and messy at the same time. Most days, it has been rewarding and fun and other days, trying and miserable. I have had so many employees that I beg to continue to serve at our restaurant for the rest of their lives. Why don't they understand that the world doesn't need another surgeon or teacher? I also have had employees that only want to work half of a shift and complain the entire time they do it.

There are always both.

You will find no staff on this planet made up entirely hard-working, motivated, reliable employees. It just does not happen. I have come very close to attaining that staff, but there would be no good without the bad. No motivation without laziness and no joy without the miserable. I have come to value my hard-workers and never take a single one of them for granted. They are my family, my rock, my support system, and the gears to the engine of a restaurant that would not run without them.

Then we have the no-shows.

Let me tell you, I am a pretty lenient boss. It takes a lot to make me upset and I long to watch people improve, therefore I am sometimes a little too patient with my employees.

Here is a list, to give you an idea, of some (in my opinion) obviously fireable offenses:

- o Not showing up for work

- o Showing up for work drunk/high/intoxicated or incoherent

- Completely ignoring and/or not complying with the rules of the restaurant

- Stealing from the job

The list goes on...

In the last year of my life I have had *six* people schedule interviews and then choose to not show up for them. I have trained two employees and then had them not show up for their first shifts. I have had someone walk out mid-shift. And I had someone wear Heelys into the restaurant to host. Heelys--those fun shoes with small wheels in the heels that you can kick out at your convenience to show society how trendy you are.

This is not a joke.

My 16-year-old hostess, Helene, barely old enough to drive a car, but old enough to know better, shows up to work, toes up, wheels out. Thinking that it was appropriate, and fashionable at that, to wear the small roller skates as a part of her uniform. I pull Helene aside and explained to her how utterly awkward it would be for her to skate our guests to their seats. I feel guilty, as I know this girl is young and she loves these shoes/skates very much.

"Helene, as long as the skates, uh, sneakers are non-slip, you may wear them with the wheels pushed in, as you are ruining our floors."

To my surprise, Helene is shocked. She sees nothing wrong with wearing skate equipment into the restaurant and is genuinely upset that I am cramping her style. After the short discussion, my hostess got the point. To everyone's surprise and relief, she stopped wearing the outrageous shoes.

I hope that somewhere in the world there is a place for them. The people who do not take their jobs seriously. The people who do not want to work. The ones who hate getting their hands dirty or working for more than three hours at a time. I'm sure they will find their place, but that place is not in a restaurant.

While letting people go may be difficult, you must do what is right for your business. Hire the ones that are going to make your place thrive and fire the ones that don't care. Surround yourself with successful, motivated individuals and their efforts will reflect your business in ways you can not even imagine. If you are an employee at a food establishment, be the right kind of worker. Show up for your shifts with a good mindset and take pride in what you do. Stick to the dress code and go buy yourself a pair of Heelys, for your days off of course.

Like I said before, managing staff is both challenging and fulfilling.

I am extremely empathetic, sensitive, emotional, and sometimes a bit of a crier (didn't think you would get to play therapist here did you?). I get very attached to the people in my life, even if I have met some of them only a handful of times. It is hard to let people go. It is weird to reprimand people that you love and care about.

I think this is something that is especially challenging as a female with authority. As women, we are naturally nurturing and protective. So, when there comes a time when we have to bear down and stand up for our businesses it can be very conflicting.

I am here to tell all my ladies out there that you do not, by any means, need to be soft spoken and polite when it comes to business, or any part of your life for that matter. If you need to demand respect, demand it and if that means letting someone go that does not have the business's best interest in mind, let them go. You are more than capable of being nurturing and affectionate, authoritative and driven at the same time in the same space.

I have learned to be the creator and the destroyer, the motherly figure and the take-no-shit manager. There is and always will be room for both.

This One's For You

This chapter is for you, the reader who has never worked in the food industry. The reader who has never come close to dropping a bowl of flaming hot soup on a newborn or given the old woman with a heart condition caffeinated coffee. The reader who loves food but hates to cook. The reader who bought this book out of the goodness of their heart and the reader who has been wondering all along if they are, in fact, the unreasonable customer in my stories.

Thank you for coming in to eat.

No matter where that may have been, you have benefitted our businesses in one way or another and for that, we are forever grateful. What would we possibly do without you?

However, you quite possibly may be on my shit-list. It is nothing personal, but if you could maybe ask for your refills at the same time instead of each time I arrive at the table with one more drink, that would help a sister out. That being said, I love you, but I have a few requests…

Manners

Please say "please" and "thank you." I know we are not children, but this is important. Whether you are in the middle of yelling at your spouse or Instagramming your appetizers, when a server picks something up, drops something off, or just checks in, show your appreciation. We are serving hot food all night long; a little kindness goes a long way.

I Forget How to Do My Job, Can You Remind Me?

Us "restaurant people" know what we are doing. It may seem to you that we are only working here for fun, but we have policies to follow, menus to memorize and money to make.

If you spot an open table but we tell you there is a 30-minute wait, please do not ask "what about right there?" as if we have completely forgotten that the table exists and are now going to seat you in front of the line of people in the waiting area. We have it under control. Patience is a virtue, especially while in public. Please try to find that inner peace that we all work so hard to attain and use it to get through that grueling half hour.

Can We All Have Separate Checks?

Someone had to bring it up. If you are one of the customers I am about to write about I sincerely apologize for any hurt feelings, however, you need to be aware of the inconvenience you have caused. It is currently 2020. We have ATMs, we have access to our banks on our phones and we have money exchange apps like Venmo, CashApp, PayPal.

I have pondered over and over in my head a nice way to ask this of our loyal customers but have honestly come up with nothing.

So here it is... stop asking for separate checks.

If it is absolutely necessary and you will never see each other again to pay each other back, then fine, we will use up our precious time splitting items between four separate bills for you and then running four separate cards and entering four separate checks.

However, if in any way avoidable, PLEASE, I am begging you, take one for the team and do not ask for separate checks. Your friends will pay you back I promise, and if not then are they really your friends? I know it doesn't seem like a problem to ask, but when a table wants ten separate checks on a Friday night at 7:00 p.m. when there are two other servers in line to use the computer and an old lady that just spilled hot coffee everywhere, it *is* the worst thing in the entire world and honestly drives us up the wall.

Wait, so This is a Real Job?!

Please do not ask us what we want to do with our lives or when we are getting "real jobs." Especially any staff that is no longer in high school. I have found this to be the most offensive and ignorant question as this IS what I want to do with my life. Many people can not fathom that serving/managing/cooking is a career but just so we're clear, we receive paychecks just like business people. We even bring home wads of cash in our bras every night! We are educated just like you, and we are actually choosing to work in this chaotic industry (believe it or not) and guess what? We are making money doing it! Just because we enjoy getting our hands dirty and working late nights does not mean we are necessarily looking for another job.

Be Nice

My last request; be kind. We appreciate every customer that enters our places of employment, as you are the reason we are here. I know you may have had bad experiences with miserable servers or rude hosts and for that, I am sorry. But we are here to serve each other and give one another a great experience, so if we could all be a little bit kinder to each other, all of our nights out would be a lot more memorable.

Come on Man, Don't Be Creepy

I have a couple that comes in every other week, let's call them Bill and Diane. Bill and Diane think they own the place. They are the first to tell anyone who will listen that they "know the owner," and they are always the last table to leave. They stop every server any chance they get to have a conversation about my family or ask questions on the status of the business. They ask with good intentions, but they are still quite annoying.

Because this couple is extremely comfortable in our space, they sometimes let comments and gestures slip out that definitely should be kept in instead.

A few months ago, Diane and Bill came in for dinner on a Friday night and Bill called me over to their table. We talked for a while before he asked me, "it seems slow in here recently is everything going alright?"

I assured him that everything was fine; August was simply a slow month with everyone on vacations, etc.

Bill laughed, "Well, maybe you should have your waitresses dress a little skimpier. That'll bring people in."

I raised my eyebrows and immediately looked at Diane who looked like she was ready to pull out divorce papers.

To Bill, and maybe to a lot of people reading this book, a joke is a joke. I get it, *don't take everything so seriously, just having a little fun, words never hurt anyone, he didn't mean it.*

The thing is this, he did mean it.

Bill had become so comfortable with me and with our restaurant that he stopped treating my staff with respect. And as I watched him mentally take back what he said I thought about all the reasons why this industry is hard to work in for anyone, but especially for women.

Bill's comment might have been a joke, but it was hurtful. It was womanizing and body-shaming and belittling all in a few words.

We know damn well, as women, that if we dress a certain way, maybe we will make more money. That does not make it right. Just because you are a waitress or a bartender or a host, you do not deserve any more or less tip money because of how much skin you show.

I was disgusted by his comment.

When Diane and Bill were finished eating, Diane came up to me and attempted to explain her husband's behavior. "I am so sorry; he was not thinking when he said that about your servers. He would never say anything like that to be hurtful, we have three daughters, you know."

I was mortified.

This man has three little girls and here he is suggesting that we wear less clothes to please men like himself so they give us more money.

I have not seen Bill or Diane in a very long time.

Whoever you are, customer, or regular or frequent flyer, please never get too comfortable. Always remember to treat your servers with respect. Put yourselves in our position and try to remember that we have lives just like you do and to treat us the way you would want your children to be treated.

There have been many various incidents in the restaurant that are equally as creepy and disrespectful as Bill's comment.

Take the rock climber for example.

We have a guy that comes in quite frequently to dine or pick up takeout. We call him the Rock Climber. This man is most likely pushing sixty and wears only turtlenecks. Already creepy, right?

So, turtleneck guy got the Rock Climber nickname by asking my 20-year-old counter girl, Amanda, if he could, you guessed it, take her rock climbing. She politely declined, using her "busy schedule" as an excuse to let the weirdo down easy.

I kid you not, Rock Climber showed up one week later and asked again, "How about you come rock climbing with me?"

My employee explained to him again that she'd rather not spend time with him outside of the restaurant, or anywhere on earth for that matter.

He seemed disappointed but still hopeful, God bless his soul.

The rock climber continues to be a regular.

However, all of my staff now know the make and model of his car, what he looks like, and can spot one of his turtlenecks from a mile away.

We make sure to hide Amanda from his god-awful invitations every time he shows up.

We get hit on. It happens everywhere, but I swear it happens more often in a restaurant setting. There is a huge difference between being polite and being a flirt and if you are an adult, or just awake, you should be able to spot the difference.

A tip for flirtatious customers out there… stop that. Just cut it out. We are adults. We are at work. We are not impressed by your kind words and creepy gestures, we are just annoyed. Show us respect while we serve you (and quite possibly your family) your dinner and we will show you respect right back.

"Any Coffee or Dessert for you Guys Tonight?"

I believe that we chose to work in the restaurant industry for one of three reasons:

1. It is a family business.

2. It is convenient for extra cash.

3. We want to push ourselves into the most insane, chaotic, booming atmosphere that we think we can handle for a while until we crack, can no longer take the heat, and very literally have to get out of the kitchen.

No matter the reason why you started, you started. Whether it was a diner serving job in college or your first high school busboy gig, you joined the club, you drank the punch. As did I.

I used to tell people that I love the restaurant industry for a hundred different reasons. I love the money, the hustle, the community, the regulars, the late nights, the chaos, etc., and I was being honest. Those aspects of this business light me up and have brought me so much happiness over the past decade of my life.

However, looking back on all the years of long hours, I realize that the reason why I love this job more than anything is that it has become my safe space. My employees are not only my employees, they are my family.

The food industry will do that to you. It might take away your Friday nights and parts of your sanity, but it will give you a home. I have many visions of what my life will become and where I will go, but I know one thing for sure, and that is the memories I have made and the person that I have become, I owe to the restaurant industry.

Thank you so much for taking the time to relate to my story and to hear my advice. I can only hope that your experience, whether a day or a decade in this business has been as exhausting, rewarding, challenging, eye-opening, and fun as mine has been.

To My People, Thank you

Thank you to my parents who built this family business and instilled my love for hard-work and commitment. My mom for teaching me how to make life beautiful when things seem ugly and for unconditionally supporting everything that I am. Thank you to my dad for telling me over and over that I will be successful in every part of my life. You have made me strong willed and confident. To my grandparents for being my loving, hilarious office-mates and my siblings (my favorite three people on earth) for keeping me motivated to be a good role model and for being my light in every dark room. Thank you to my regulars who believed in me from day one and who keep me sane on the shittiest of nights. I am so so appreciative of every one of you, you are the reason why this business is so rewarding. Thank you to my girlfriends, who understand my workaholic tendencies and keep me the weirdest, realest version of myself at all times. Thank you to Matt (former bus boy turned lover). For pushing me to do everything I know I can and never letting me give up on what I want, I love you and will forever be your dinner date. Most of all thank you to my staff. For teaching me how to be a boss, how to delegate, how to not mess up the schedule (too horribly) and for showing me respect. You have all unknowingly given me so much confidence in myself and I would not be the person I am today without you people. Thank you thank you thank you, I love you guys.

Made in the USA
Columbia, SC
05 June 2020